W9-DJG-829

Rookie Read-About® Science

Life in a Tide Pool

By Allan Fowler

Consultants
Linda Cornwell, Learning Resource Consultant,
Indiana Department of Education

Fay Robinson, Child Development Specialist

Lynne Kepler, Educational Consultant

Children's Press®
A Division of Grolier Publishing
New York   London   Hong Kong   Sydney
Danbury, Connecticut

Project Editor: Downing Publishing Services
Designer: Herman Adler Design Group
Photo Researcher: Caroline Anderson

Library of Congress Cataloging-in-Publication Data

Fowler, Allan.
    Life in a tide pool / by Allan Fowler.
      p. cm. – (Rookie read-about science)
    Includes index.
    Summary: Explains how tidal pools form and the types of plants and
animals that inhabit them.
    ISBN 0-516-20031-3 (lib. bdg.) — ISBN 0-516-26083-9 (pbk.)
    1. Tide pool ecology—Juvenile literature. [1. Tide pool ecology.
    2. Ecology.] I. Title. II. Series.
QH531.5.S35F68   1996
574.5'2636–dc20   96-13894
                                                  CIP
                                                  AC

These young people are
exploring a tide pool.

You can get a close look
at many kinds of ocean
life in a tide pool.

Tide pools are small pools of ocean water found in rocky places along the seashore.

How do they get there?

Twice a day, the water gets higher and higher. This is called high tide.

And twice a day, the water
flows back to the sea. This
is low tide. At low tide,
you can see rocks that were
covered by water at high tide.

Not all the water flows
back when the tide goes
out. Some of it remains.

It fills holes in the rocks
or hollow spaces between
rocks. These small bodies
of water are tide pools.

starfish

When the tide rises, it carries many sea animals right up to the rocks.

Most of them are swept back into the ocean when the tide goes out.

But others are left behind in tide pools. Once there, some of them never leave.

Barnacles, for instance.

A barnacle attaches
itself to the rocks around
a tide pool . . .

grows a hard shell . . .

and stays there for the
rest of its life.

barnacles

Barnacles also attach themselves to ships, or whales, or any solid surface.

Mussels, too, attach themselves to solid surfaces. These mussels and barnacles have collected on pilings.

You might find shellfish such
as limpets or mussels . . .

mussels

snails

or snails or crabs . . .
clinging to the rocks
around a tide pool.

Sea anemones look like plants, but they are animals and can move around.

sea anemone

starfish

Starfish often live in tide pools. Most kinds of starfish have five arms, though some have ten or more.

A sea urchin, with its
spines, might remind
you of a porcupine.

sea urchins

What do all these animals eat? Mostly plankton.

Plankton is a mass of very tiny animals, and simple plants called algae, floating in the sea.

The incoming tide brings plankton to the tide pool.

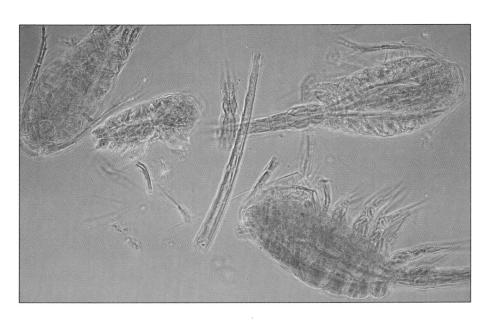

plankton

Plants such as Irish moss and sea lettuce grow on the rocks in tide pools.

sea lettuce

rockweed

Kelp and rockweed grow
there, too. People usually
call all these kinds of
plants seaweed.

Tide pools are fun
to explore.

You never know what
living creatures might
come in on the next
high tide.

Words You Know

high tide

low tide

Irish moss

kelp

rockweed

sea lettuce

barnacles

crab

limpets

mussels

plankton

sea urchins

snails

starfish

tide pool

31

Index

About the Author

Allan Fowler is a free-lance writer with a background in advertising.
Born in New York, he lives in Chicago now and enjoys traveling.

Photo Credits

Visuals Unlimited — ©Dave B. Fleetham, cover; ©Steve McCutcheon, 16;
©Mack Henley, 18, 19, 31 (center left), 31 (bottom left); ©Daniel W. Gotshall,
21, 28; ©David M. Phillips, 25 (top); ©John D. Cunningham, 25 (bottom),
30 (center left), 31 (center middle); ©Hal Beral, 30 (center right)

Norbert Wu — ©Brandon Cole/Mo Yung Productions, 3

Valan Photos — ©Roy Luckow, 5, 12, 31 (bottom middle); ©Joyce Photographics,
6, 31 (bottom right); ©Francis Lepine, 8, 30 (top left); ©Stephen J. Krasemann,
9, 22, 30 (top right); ©Pam Hickman, 10; ©James R. Page, 11, 23, 31 (top right),
31 (center right); ©Herman H. Giethoorn, 15, 27, 30 (bottom left), 31 (top left);
©T. Joyce, 26, 30 (bottom right); ©Alan Wilkinson, 31 (top middle)

COVER: Boy in tide pool with slate-pencil sea urchins